Can We Get That Here?

by Donna Foley

**Property of
Kindred Public School**

Editorial Offices: Glenview, Illinois • Parsippany, New Jersey • New York, New York
Sales Offices: Needham, Massachusetts • Duluth, Georgia • Glenview, Illinois
Coppell, Texas • Ontario, California • Mesa, Arizona

Different crops grow in different parts of the country. In the summer many kinds of fruits and vegetables may grow near where you live. Some of these local foods might be sold at a farmer's market. Foods that are not grown locally might be available to you only at a grocery store.

Many climates are good for growing fruits and vegetables. In most areas fruits and vegetables are harvested from May through October. Farmers are **producers** who sell their fruits and vegetables to **consumers**, both locally and all over the country.

Your family might make a shopping list every week. This list could change during the year because different foods are available in different places at different times.

In the winter months the foods that grow in warmer climates may not be as easy to find. The farmer's market is usually closed, but you may still be able to buy your favorite fruits and vegetables at the grocery store. Farmers in warmer climates ship their foods to stores in colder climates. This way, you can almost always find everything on your list!

Oranges are one example of a food that comes from a warmer climate. Oranges grow in Florida, where it is warm for almost the whole year. The farmers who grow oranges sell their crops to distributors. Distributors are people who sell the oranges to grocery stores and deliver them there. Once the food is in the stores, you can buy what you need. Often, fruits and vegetables have to travel great distances to get to your grocery store. Farmers and distributors work together to get food to you from all over the country!

Potatoes are another food that might have to travel to get to you and your family. Potatoes are an important crop in Idaho, which is in the western part of the United States. Just as with oranges, farmers and distributors work together to get potatoes to a store near you. You then can eat baked potatoes, mashed potatoes, or potato pancakes!

Foods ripen and become ready to eat only during certain times of the year. Cherries, for example, are picked in June and July. Asparagus has a very short growing season. Each food has a special growing season, making it easier to get during some months of the year.

Many foods grow during the spring and summer and are ready to be harvested in the fall. Pears, apples, and corn are just a few of these foods. The Thanksgiving holiday celebrates the fact that so many foods are available during this season and that people are thankful for them. Pumpkin, beans, and squash are some of the foods that people especially enjoy when the weather turns cooler.

Farmers are busy harvesting their crops in the fall, but they are also busy in the spring. The spring is when crops are planted and young plants start to grow. There is a lot to do to get the fields and soil ready. After the seeds are planted, there are many other jobs to do while the crops grow. The farmers look forward to harvest time and to enjoying the foods that come from their crops!

    You may have friends or family members who do not live near you. Different foods may grow where they live. The climates and growing seasons may be different.

    It is fun to send or receive food from other places as a gift. You might get peaches or pecans from South Carolina, grapefruits from Florida, or mangoes from Mexico. It is possible for you and your family to enjoy foods from all over the world!

No matter how you get these foods, it is fun to enjoy them with others. You and your family may have special dishes from your culture that you share with others. It can be fun to prepare foods that are made from all these different fruits and vegetables. Your family can eat these treats, made with foods from all over, as part of a special meal.

Foods can come from many places. You can get them at a grocery store, at a farmer's market, or even in your own backyard. The next time you sit down for a special dinner, take a moment to think about how those foods were grown and how they made it to your table.

Glossary

consumer someone who buys and uses goods

crop a kind of plant that people grow and use

producer someone who makes or grows something